AFFILIATE MARKETING

The Guide To Digital Success Using SEO And Social Media Marketing Efficiently

Timothy Bell

© Copyright 2020 by Timothy Bell - All rights reserved.

The follow eBook is reproduced below with the goal of providing information that is as accurate and reliable as possible. Regardless, purchasing this eBook can be seen as consent to the fact that both the publisher and the author of this book are in no way experts on the topics discussed within and that any recommendations or suggestions that are made herein are for entertainment purposes only. Professionals should be consulted as needed prior to undertaking any of the action endorsed herein.

This declaration is deemed fair and valid by both the American Bar Association and the Committee of Publishers Association and is legally binding throughout the United States.

Furthermore, the transmission, duplication or reproduction of any of the following work including specific information will be considered an illegal act irrespective of if it is done electronically or in print. This extends to creating a secondary or tertiary copy of the work or a recorded copy and is only allowed with express written consent from the Publisher. All additional right reserved.

The information in the following pages is broadly considered to be a truthful and accurate account of facts and as such any inattention, use or misuse of the information in question by the reader will render any resulting actions solely under their purview. There are no scenarios in which the publisher or the original author of this work can be in any fashion deemed liable for any hardship or damages that may befall them after undertaking information described herein.

Additionally, the information in the following pages is intended only for informational purposes and should thus be thought of as universal. As befitting its nature, it is presented without assurance regarding its prolonged validity or interim quality. Trademarks that are mentioned are done without written consent and can in no way be considered an endorsement from the trademark holder.

Table of Contents

Introduction 5

Chapter 1: Introduction To Affiliate Marketing 7
   Fundamentals Of Affiliate Marketing 8
   Content Creation 9
   Finding A Niche 10
   How Affiliate Marketing Works 11
   How to Make Money From Affiliate Marketing............... 12

Chapter 2: Getting Started In The World Of Affiliate Marketing 15
   Deciding On An Aim... 16
   How To Determine Your Aim... 17
   Choosing The Right Channel... 18
   Putting It All Together.. 21

Chapter 3: Finding Your Niche 23
   Identifying Your Product.. 23
   Identifying Your Target Audience...................................... 24
   Delivering Your Value Proposition 26
   Establishing Your Niche... 27

Chapter 4: Making Sales Happen 29
   Generating Rapport... 30
   Get Personal With Your Audience 30
   Making Product Reviews Engaging 31
   Use Reliable Sources 32
   Choose Products And Brands Carefully 33
   Develop A Consistent Approach... 34
   Stay Current... 35
   Sponsored Posts 35

Chapter 5: Building An Online Presence 37
   Becoming A Blogger 38
   Mailing Lists 39
   Social Media 40
   Video Streaming 43

Chapter 6: Best Sites For Affiliate Marketing 45
   Amazon Associates 45
   eBay Partners 46
   Shopify Affiliates 47
   Rakuten Affiliates 47
   Clickbank 48
   ShareASale 48
   Solvid Affiliates 49
   Google AdSense 49
   Choosing The Best Affiliate Site 50

Chapter 7: Introduction To Search Engine Optimization 51
   Fundamentals Of SEO 52
   Crawl Accessibility 53
   Compelling Material 54
   Keyword Heavy 55
   User Experience 56
   Great Content 56
   Click-through Rates 57
   Snippets or Schema Results 58

Chapter 8: Leveraging Social Media 60
   Defining a Social Media Strategy 60
   Getting Started 62
   Posting Content 63
   Case Study 64
   Bringing it All Together 65

Conclusion 67

Introduction

Congratulations on purchasing Affiliate Marketing: The guide to digital success using SEO and social media marketing efficiently. and thank you for doing so.

The following chapters will discuss the fundamentals of affiliate marketing.

Have you been looking to get started in the world of affiliate marketing but don't know where to start?

Have you been looking for a clear and concise guide that can help you get started making serious money online?

Have you been looking for a serious approach to affiliate marketing without having to spend thousands of dollars on courses?

Have you been looking for a proven method that can help you get started quickly and easily?

If you can relate to any of these questions, then this is the book for you. In this guide, you will find the best approach to affiliate marketing. Best of all, it's written in a way that's straight to the point. There are no esoteric approaches here.

In this volume, you will find the knowledge you need in order to get started making money through affiliate marketing. You will learn about the best ways in which you can make money while avoiding the most common pitfalls. Plus, you will find real-life examples.

This is a clear and straightforward guide to making money through affiliate market. Best of all, you don't need any prior knowledge. You already have the most important know-how.

So, if you are serious about making money by leveraging the power of social media and e-commerce, this is the book for you. You will find the right content you need right from the start. This isn't about stringing readers along until they get to some cheesy sales pitch. This is the real deal, insider information you won't find in a single volume.

Chapter 1:
Introduction To Affiliate Marketing

Affiliate marketing is a branch of digital marketing. Digital marketing emerged with the rise of the internet. As companies and advertisers realized that marketing was moving away from traditional mass media (television, radio, and print), an entirely new field of marketing was born.

In its infancy, digital marketing replicated traditional mass media advertising. In these early days, ads moved from print to digital media. For instance, text-heavy blogs were a staple of early digital marketing efforts.

As video streaming and social media burst onto the scene, advertisers realized that they too could capitalize on these media platforms. As a result, digital marketing took on a new dimension. Moreover, the public slowly began to move away from traditional advertising. This was the direct result of social media taking over.

At present, traditional media is still prevalent. Television ad space is just as coveted as in the past. The difference is that digital marketing has taken over the landscape. Therefore, digital media are the first stop for anyone looking to consume products and services.

That being said, affiliate marketing was born from traditional digital marketing. Brands began to view influencers and internet celebrities as assets they could leverage to promote their brands thereby generating sales. It's important to note that this isn't about traditional celebrity endorsements. We're talking about regular people who can leverage their skills and talents for the purpose of promoting brands, products, or services.

Consequently, affiliate marketing provided both brands and consumers a new way of interacting with one another. This is all made possible by the work done by content creators. As such, it's content creators who facilitate this interaction.

Fundamentals Of Affiliate Marketing

In essence, affiliate marketing consists of earning a commission as a result of promoting a brand. Generally speaking, this can happen directly or indirectly. It's also important to note that a brand does not actively promote itself. Rather, the content creator is the one who promotes the brand. In exchange, they receive a commission for their efforts.

Thus, brands do not produce any of the content themselves, at least not publicly. It's the content creators who leverage a brand's popularity. This dynamic allows both content creators and brands to use each other's popularity.

Consider this example:

A well-known internet celebrity shares beauty and fashion tips with her followers. She regularly posts blogs entries, videos, or social media content in which she features certain brands that she uses. To make money from this effort, she provides a link in which followers can purchase the items she has used. When a follower clicks on the link and makes a purchase, the content creator receives a cut from the sale. This cut comes in the form of a sales commission. Depending on the brand or e-commerce site, the payout could be weekly or monthly.

That is affiliate marketing in a nutshell.

However, there's a lot more that goes on behind the scenes.

First of all, not all brands or e-commerce platforms engage in affiliate marketing. As such, it's crucial to know which brands and sites offer this option. From there, content creators can choose who to sign up with. Once this new partnership has been started, content creators can begin to reap the rewards of this scheme.

Content Creation

This is the hard part.

Successful affiliate marketing boils down to creating useful and engaging content. This is what drives marketing efforts. The main idea is to expose the brand(s) to as many potential customers as possible. This is why the internet enables content creators to infinitely scale their creations.

There is no single platform or media that's better than others. The choice of media is related to the type of content being produced. For instance, some content is suited for visual representation such as workout videos. Other types of content are suited for a text-based format such as novels.

Your choice of media boils down to the specific niche you are targeting. This is why you need to have a clear idea in your mind about what you are planning to do, who you are going to target, and what you are looking to achieve.

Please keep in mind that you may need to learn some specific skills to produce content. This might mean learning video production and editing skills. You may also have to brush up on your writing skills. Moreover, you may have to invest in equipment to produce content. While none of this is a prerequisite, you may find yourself needing to go down this route eventually.

Finding A Niche

Finding your niche is a crucial decision in affiliate marketing. Making the wrong choice can lead to fruitless labor. On the other hand, making the right choice can lead to a highly profitable endeavor. Choosing your niche boils down to your ability to leverage your knowledge, talents, skills, and experience. For example, if you are a skilled baker, starting a channel dedicated to baking would make sense. In contrast, it would be pointless to start a music review channel if you have little knowledge of the topic.

Another way that affiliate marketers go about finding their niche is by following their hearts. Successful marketers engage in activities they are passionate about even if they know little about it. In this regard, content creators go on a journey in which they share their passion with their audience. In the end, sales are driven by the engagement from followers.

Lastly, some marketers seek the most profitable niches. Often, this means producing content that's aimed specifically to a product, brand, or industry. Nevertheless, the point is not to produce content from the heart. Rather, the aim is to produce content that resonates with a specific type of audience. In the end, the idea is to drive sales.

At this point, it's a good idea for you to begin thinking about the type of niche you would like to focus on. Keep these ideas in mind as we have an entire chapter dedicated to the process of determining your niche. For now, having some ideas about what niches you'd like to pursue is a great way to start.

How Affiliate Marketing Works

Affiliate marketing is a rather straightforward process. There are no complex formulas or processes. This is why so many folks seek to become a part of this marketing scheme. Here is an overview of how the process works.

The process begins with choosing a niche and media to present content. This process is the necessary groundwork that leads to generating sales which in turn generates income. Also, content creators need to sign up with the brand or e-commerce site. Now, here is what happens once content has been loaded to the platform of choice.

1. The creator posts content. Users and followers interact with the content. The creator needs to ensure that there are links to the products they are advertising. These links can be found in the post. The content should enable users to click on the links so they can check out the products or services advertised in the content.

2. Users click on the link that redirects them to the brand's site. This could also be an e-commerce platform such as e-Bay or Amazon. The system logs the referral coming directly from the content creator.

3. When the user makes a purchase using the affiliate's link, the system logs this sale as coming from an affiliate (content creator). The system validates the purchase and credits the sale to the affiliate.

4. Once the sale has been validated, the corresponding commission is credited to the affiliate's account. The total account is credited up to the point of payout. Payout periods vary from site to site.

5. At the payout date, the site issues payment in whatever fashion they deem appropriate. At this point, the content creator is paid for their referrals.

That's the way affiliate marketing works.

The entire system is automated and dependent on the number of valid sales. For instance, if a user clicks on the link in the affiliate's content but does not make the sale, the affiliate does not earn any revenue. If the user purchases the item later on but does not click on the affiliate's link, then the affiliate does not earn any revenue. This is why content creators always urge their customers to help them by using their link to purchase the products advertised in the content.

It's worth noting that some sites don't payout unless a certain quota is met. This is why you need to read the fine print. This will alert you on the terms and conditions you can expect. Moreover, some sites don't pay out until after a certain amount of time. For example, the site may not pay until a three-month period of membership.

How to Make Money From Affiliate Marketing

There are three basic ways in which you can make money through affiliate marketing. You can focus any one of these ways or all three.

Sales commissions

You can earn commissions as described in the process above. This is the most common way in which affiliates make money. However, it's worth considering the rates paid out by brands. On the whole, these rates vary.

Generally speaking, commission rates can range from 1% to 10%. More aggressive brands may be willing to pay up to 10%

while more established brands may fall somewhere closer to the 1% to 3% mark. The industry average is roughly 4% to 5%. This may not seem like much, but when multiplied by a high volume of sales, commissions can certainly become profitable.

When you are looking to sign up with a brand, make sure to double-check the rate they pay. Some brands have a tiered rate system. So, top earners make a higher commission rate while newbies must work their way up. There may be additional bonuses or rewards depending on the volume of sales. Some of these incentives include additional payouts, free products, or extra promotion.

Commissions on leads

Depending on the type of product or service, affiliates may receive a commission for the leads they generate. This type of scheme is used when the product has a high value, or the brand has its own sales team. A good example of this is real estate. Realtors are willing to pay a commission for good leads. It's important to note that realtors only payout when the deals close. Therefore, generating leads is a matter of finding prospective buyers for specific properties.

Generating income from leads can be a good source of income if you can find potential customers for other companies. Depending on the nature of the product or service, this can be quite profitable. So, do take the time to consider this option.

Pay per click

Some affiliates get paid for directing traffic to someone else's website, blog, social media, or video streaming channel. Each time a user clicks on a link provided by the affiliate, the affiliate receives a payout. Often, the payout is less than a penny per click. However, a high volume of traffic can be mean hundreds if not thousands of dollars for each payout. In this scheme, content creators produce enticing content that keeps users coming back. The content creator may place banners, buttons, or links to the other brand's site.

This type of affiliate marketing is popular with publishers. For instance, news sites use affiliates to help promote their media platforms. Also, video streaming services use this type of scheme to drive traffic. If you are considering this type of scheme, then please keep in mind you need to publish content quite frequently.

As you can see, there are several ways in which you can make money through affiliate marketing. If you can find a niche that can leverage all three sources, you can clean up. However, most marketers choose to focus on these areas individually. So, they create content specifically geared toward that type of affiliate marketing scheme. This might involve creating separate content. In the end, having multiple sources of revenue far outweighs the time and effort invested in developing great content.

Chapter 2:
Getting Started In The World Of Affiliate Marketing

When getting started with affiliate marketing, it's important to think about the reasons behind your efforts. Lots of folks out there believe that affiliate marketing is as easy as writing a blog or posting videos on YouTube. The fact is that being a successful affiliate marketer requires some careful thought. By taking the time to think carefully about what you hope to achieve from affiliate marketing, you'll go a long way.

That's why this chapter is dedicated to laying the foundation for your affiliate marketing endeavors. In particular, when you make a concerted effort in planning your projects, you'll make things much easier for yourself down the road. This is why the planning stage is the most important part of your affiliate marketing plan. As you lay out everything you plan to do, you'll take the guesswork out of your activities.

This is what successful marketers do. They plan everything out before making a single piece of content. Being aware of your end game is the most important thing you can do during the planning stage. By having a clear understanding of your end game, you will be able to carry out the activities needed to achieve it.

So, let's get started laying down the solid foundation for what will eventually become a successful affiliate marketing plan.

Deciding On An Aim

The first question to address pertains to your aims. In short, you need to define what you hope to achieve. There are different reasons why folks become involved in affiliate marketing. So, let's take a look at some of them.

Generate passive earnings

One of the most coveted results of affiliate marketing is "passive income." This type of income refers to the revenues you earn without having to actively work for it. While this doesn't mean "free" money, it does mean that you work once and get paid over and over.

When you create effective content, more and more users interact with it. Thus, this enables you to generate steady revenue from a single task. Additionally, the more engaging content you produce, the more passive income you stand to generate.

In essence, passive income is about making money while you sleep. This is true because your content continues to work while you don't. Passive income allows you to dedicate your time to other endeavors while still generating earnings.

Flexible work

This is the biggest reason why affiliate marketing is so appealing. You can set up your marketing efforts anywhere, anytime. As a result, you don't have to take on another job to make money through affiliate marketing. You can produce content in your free time. This means that you can do it on top of any other activities you are currently engaging in.

Furthermore, affiliate marketing allows you to work anywhere. If you are keen on hitting the road, you can create content anywhere in the world. However, it's important to note that you need to be consistent. Successful marketers consistently post new content. Otherwise, any momentum you gain may be lost. So, being consistent is crucial to your success.

Cost-effectiveness

It's surprisingly cost-effective to get started in affiliate marketing. You can begin with modest tools and build your way up. While you may need to invest in your content at some point, you don't need to make any significant upfront investment. Depending on the type of content you produce, all you might needs is a computer and an internet connection.

Affiliate marketing is the type of endeavor that you can start with virtually no money. The most important capital you need is your creativity. As such, your success boils down to your unique way of delivering valuable content to your users. If done right, it can produce great results. So, affiliate marketing can prove to be a great way to make money with little to no investment.

How To Determine Your Aim

At this point, it's important to consider what your aim is. Ask yourself the following questions:

1. What do I want to achieve?
2. Who do I want to reach?
3. How much do I want to earn?

These three questions will lead you toward developing a roadmap to success. Please take the time to answer them honestly. Honest answers will lead you to devise a realistic plan. Otherwise, you'll lack the vision needed to develop a coherent strategy.

When considering what you want to achieve, be honest. If you aspire to make a living from affiliate marketing, then be prepared to devote considerable time and effort in perfecting your craft. Making a full-time living from affiliate marketing demands careful thought and consideration. On the other hand, if you're only looking to make some extra cash, then you can create content in your free time.

Also, consider your audience. Determining your target audience boils down to figuring out who consumes the products you are promoting. For instance, if you're targeting a younger audience, then your content needs to be appealing to kids and teens. If you're looking to target older folks, then your content needs to be relevant to the lives of these people. You can learn a lot about your target audience by researching the products and brands you promote. This will provide you with plenty of information and insight into your target audience.

Additionally, think about how much you want to earn. Affiliate marketing has unlimited earning potential. This means that the sky is the limit. However, the more you plan to earn, the more you need to hone your craft. Successful marketers are innovative and consistent. If you can innovatively deliver consistent value, you'll surely generate revenue. However, if you end up getting stuck in a rut, you'll quickly fall out of favor with your audience.

Choosing The Right Channel

Your choice of the channel makes all the difference between success and failure. This decision is dependent on the type of content you plan to deliver. Therefore, the right channel will effectively deliver the content. The wrong choice may prove to be detrimental to the content itself.

Consider this situation:

You are planning on delivering sewing and knitting tips. You aim to promote brands related to home projects, sewing, knitting, and other related DIY projects. You intend to produce content that shows users how to produce their DIY projects.

To deliver your content, you choose to start a blog. So, your content is text-heavy, utilizes some images, and provides step-by-step instructions. On the whole, the blog is nicely done. It also offers a pleasing visual to users. However, it's text-heavy and does not provide an easy-to-follow approach. As a result, the blog doesn't get as many hits.

The mistake here is delivering visual content in a text-heavy format. A great of turning this content around would be to produce video demos of how the projects should be completed. In this regard, you could embed a video to your blog post. Users can then read the blog post and watch the video or jump directly to the video.

This approach creates a lot more engagement. In the end, users are then directed to a link where they can pick up the products you used in the project.

As you can see, the channel that you use can determine the effectiveness of your content. This is why we're going to explore the following channels.

Video content

This is the first channel that comes to mind. Affiliate marketers love to exploit video channels such as YouTube as it provides a free platform. When marketers achieve a solid following, they can become influencers. Influencers are individuals who have a large following among internet users. These influencers can then leverage their popularity to promote brands, products, or services. In some cases, brands may reach out directly to influencers to offer them sponsored videos.

Video content generally needs to be produced clearly and maintain a certain consistency. Videos that are poorly shot or unedited may turn off users. So, it's best to learn some basic production and editing skills. As you gain more and more experience, you can then produce better-quality videos.

Blogs and books

Another common approach is producing text-based content. This type of content may come in the form of blogs, articles, or books. Often, these contents provide detailed information about a topic that is related to certain brands. As such, users are encouraged to check out the links provided in the content itself.

It's worth noting that text-based content needs to be engaging and valuable. Otherwise, it will be quite difficult for users to engage with the content effectively. Moreover, users may be unmotivated to follow links to products, and so on.

If you are considering this avenue, you may need to hire the services of a professional copywriter. Otherwise, you may have to brush up on your writing skills. Being authentic is important, too. So, keep this in mind. Successful marketers deliver useful content time and again.

Social media

Influencers make a living from social media. Instagram is the go-to platform when it comes to social media marketing. The reason for this lies in its visual-first nature. Instagram is a great way of using visuals to showcase products and brands.

Other social media platforms depend on the type of product being promoted. Facebook offers a balanced approach between text and image. Also, Facebook is marketed toward an older audience. LinkedIn is exclusively marketed toward professionals while other social media platforms tend to cater to niche segments.

If you are planning on using social media intensively, please bear in mind that you need to deliver constant and consistent content. You cannot expect posts to be evergreen. Moreover, in the social media world, you're only as good as your last post. This is why social media celebrities try outrageous gimmicks to keep their engagement up.

Putting It All Together

By now, you have all the elements you need to build a winning strategy. When you put careful consideration into the elements outlined herein, you can build a winning game plan. Most importantly, putting time and effort into producing useful content is the key to success. It doesn't matter what the content is, it just needs to resonate with your target audience. If you fail to hit home, your content may fail to click.

So, here is a rundown of what you need to take into consideration when devising your strategy:

1. Decide on an aim
2. Choose the right channel
3. Determine the target audience
4. Planning content

With these four steps, you can begin to plan the way your affiliate marketing strategy will look like. As a result, you will be able to articulate a plan that reflects your aims. Otherwise, you risk being all over the place. When you fail to convey a clear message to your audience, you will confuse them. They may find your content useful or amusing, but they won't see the connection to your aim. Thus, communicating a clear intention is crucial when it comes to building a successful affiliate marketing scheme.

Lastly, it's important to consider the impact that you plan to have on the brands you are promoting. If you paint brands in an unfavorable light, you may end up creating the opposite effect. This is why product reviews, opinions, tests, tryouts, and so on, need to be carefully done. "Unbiased" opinions are always skewed toward promoting a specific product. This is why you need to make sure that you don't inadvertently trash a product you are looking to promote.

Please keep in mind that talking bad about competitors is a no-no. Trashing the competition is a sure-fire way to get booted from most platforms. So, stick to your forte. Convey your message to your audience as much as you can. It's also important, to be honest. Tell your audience to click on the link. By doing so, they are helping you deliver the content they enjoy. As such, there is no shame in nudging your audience to hit those links.

Chapter 3:
Finding Your Niche

A common misconception of novice affiliate marketers is that their content must have a universal appeal. The fact is that affiliate marketing is highly segmented. This means that you need to focus on a specific target audience. Otherwise, your efforts will not resonate as effectively as they could.

Finding your niche in affiliate marketing is about understanding what your product or service is about. This implies finding out who is interested in it. Moreover, it's about knowing what type of content your audience is interested in receiving. When you put these elements together, you can deliver a value proposition that will lead to sales.

It's important to focus on delivering value. The most successful marketers deliver value to their audience consistently. Therefore, it's crucial to produce quality content regularly. This is the key to successful affiliate marketing. If you are unable to produce quality content, your results may be disappointing.

That is why we're going to be focusing on finding your niche, how to capitalize on it, and how to keep them engaged. When you achieve these aims, you can obtain the results that you have set your sights on.

Identifying Your Product

In theory, you could market any product or service. The fundamentals are the same regardless of the specific segment you target. However, it's not quite so simple. When starting with affiliate marketing, it's best to stick to a product you are familiar with. Doing so will make the learning curve a lot easier to handle. In particular, you won't need to spend time learning how the product works or how you can target your audience effectively.

The first step is to find a product or service that you know well. This could be anything. For instance, if you are familiar with makeup and fashion, this could be your angle. Also, if you are familiar with watches and jewelry, you could find your product in this segment.

The main thing to keep in mind is that you must be knowledgeable. You can't afford to seem foolish when promoting your product. Sure, you may not know everything there is to know, but having a solid understanding of the product goes a long way.

In general, most marketers exploit their job experience. For example, if you're a lawyer, you could provide legal tips utilizing a blog. The blog then generates traffic or leads for law firms. This is a way you can transform your credibility and experience into affiliate marketing success.

Identifying Your Target Audience

Once you have a product in mind, the next step is to identify your target audience. To do this, you need to ask, "who can benefit from this product?" This answer to this question will lead you to determine who your target audience will be. Please bear in mind that you must be as specific as you possibly can. Having a clear idea of who you're targeting will make all the difference.

Here are the criteria you need to consider when determining your target audience:

- Age
- Income
- Socioeconomic status (working, middle, upper class)
- Type of brand (commercial, luxury, niche)
- Sales cycle (how long it takes to make a sale on average)
- Sales volume (number of units sold)
- Price
- Frequency of purchase
- Need (a problem they need to solve)

These criteria should give you a clear picture of who you are targeting with your content. Then, it is advisable for you to craft a description of the average individual you are targeting. For instance, "males aged 40-59, middle to upper class, professional or self-employed, seeking to find alternative sources of entertainment."

This description is consistent with middle-aged males seeking to broaden their horizons. So, your value proposition could lie in providing content about extreme sports, vacation spots, thrill-seeking activities, and so on. Therefore, your content should be geared toward promoting brands related to outdoor equipment, sports gear, travel arrangements among other types of entertainment activities.

In contrast, it would be a mistake to promote a line of fashion items such as shoes or jewelry as these are not consistent with extreme or outdoor activities. Ultimately, you're looking to deliver value in the form of information that your target audience can put to use or benefit from.

Let's consider another example.

You describe your target audience as, "females, aged 20 to 35, working-class, interested in fitness and health, little time to go to the gym, living on a tight budget."

In this description, you are making it clear that these are females who are working, have little time to go to the gym, and have a tight budget. As such, your content might be focused on providing exercise and nutrition tips. The brands and products could range from exercise equipment to fashion all aimed at a lower income bracket.

As you can see, having a clear definition of your target audience can help you line up your content strategy. As such, your content should be geared toward engaging your audience so that they keep coming back for more. When successful, your target audience will see themselves in your content. This link helps users coming back while also attracting others.

Delivering Your Value Proposition

Generally speaking, the ultimate value that your followers get, comes from the products they buy. However, the key to making these sales comes from the value proposition you are delivering. This proposition is based on helping your followers see the value in the content you deliver. If your content does not deliver value, then it will not generate the engagement you seek.

So, in addition to identifying your target audience, it's important to make your value proposition clear in your content. You should not expect audiences to perceive it for themselves. Now, this isn't about dumbing things down for people. It's just a question of simplifying the process. After all, you shouldn't expect audiences to figure your value proposition for themselves. You'll save yourself time and effort by telling them about it.

For example, if your content is based on wholesome nutrition, your followers can expect to find useful information that will help them stay healthy. This is something your followers will figure out for themselves. However, it makes things easier for everyone if you tell them that you're delivering them useful information on nutrition and wellbeing. This is how you can position yourself, and your content, in the minds of your followers.

Establishing Your Niche

By putting all of these elements together, you will be ready to hit your niche. It's always a good idea to explicitly describe what your niche is. For example, your niche could be the "luxury vintage watch market." This is a highly specialized niche. So, you shouldn't expect to get thousands upon thousands of hits. You might only get a few hundred hits in a specific time frame. But you know that those hits represent followers who may end up making large purchases.

In contrast, your niche might be a lot broader, something like the "brand new fashion sneaker market." In this niche, you are not going to be talking about sports. Rather, your focus will be on providing fashion advice on how to look good, popular brands, among other relevant information.

However, there is one important consideration to keep in mind. Always take a look at the competition in your chosen niche. If you happen to choose an unexplored or underserved niche, then you might find it easier to get your foot in the door.

On the contrary, if you try to enter a niche that's already packed with established individuals, then you might have a harder time breaking through.

When looking to enter a competitive niche, you need to figure out an innovative angle to your content. This means that you need to make yourself stand out from the rest. This could be done in a myriad of ways. Whatever approach you choose, it has to be engaging with your target audience. Otherwise, your content may fall flat and get lost among the sea of competitors.

Also, please keep in mind the types of brands you are looking to promote. If you are attempting to enter a luxury product niche, you shouldn't expect to engage audiences with ridiculous antics. Rather, you would need to stand out by producing content that's in line with the brand's philosophy. Otherwise, you'll send mixed signals.

Once you have determined your niche, target audience, and value proposition, you are ready to begin making content. It's essential that you look into what other competitors are doing prior to producing anything. This will help you get an idea of what others are doing. By studying successful marketers, you can pick ideas to help you at the beginning. From there, you can develop your value proposition so that you can stand out from the rest of the pack. In the end, your choice of content will give you the leverage you need to become a successful affiliate marketer. Please keep in mind that this is a process. So, achieving instant, overnight success is somewhat unrealistic.

Chapter 4:
Making Sales Happen

The whole point of affiliate marketing is to make sales. Of course, you can become a celebrity thereby garnering endorsement deals. As a matter of fact, this is a logical progression from regular affiliate marketing. When your persona, or your brand, takes off, other brands will look to you as a means of promoting their agenda.

At the outset, generating traffic and making sales is the most important thing you need to pursue. Thus, the content you produce ought to be directed at compelling users to use your links or your codes to make purchases.

In a sense, being an affiliate marketer is like being a salesperson. Your content needs to showcase the products you are selling. Thus, you must create a personal brand or persona that you can leverage for this purpose.

Creating a persona may imply using your real identity or concocting a fictitious one. Now, we're not talking about fooling people. But rather than being "Mary Smith," you can be the "Purse Lady." Audiences tend to resonate more with a character as this reveals the intentions behind the content.

In this chapter, we are going to look at ways in which you can develop your brand. Whether you choose to use your real identity or come up with an entirely new one, these guidelines will help you be successful at making sales happen.

Generating Rapport

Rapport boils down to establishing a relationship with your audience. They need to see themselves reflected in you. The easiest way to do this is by sharing passions and interests. When your audience sees that you like the same things, they will be compelled to follow you. When this occurs, your audience will trust you.

Additionally, it's important to position yourself as an expert. Now, this isn't about telling your audience how smart you are. It's about showing them that you know what you are talking about. This is why it's important to start with products that you are familiar with. The last thing you want is for users to call you out due to your lack of knowledge.

When you establish rapport, your audience will take you at face value. So, if you recommend a product, they'll try it out because you said so. As a result, you need to check out products before you recommend them. Otherwise, recommending bad products will quickly trash your content's traction.

Please keep in mind that sticking to your niche is crucial. There needs to be a consistency in the types of products and brands you are talking about. Showcasing a vast array of products will not position you in your niche. You may confuse your audience. Consequently, your content won't gain the traction that you need to convert sales.

Get Personal With Your Audience

Sharing generic information won't cut it. In today's digital marketing landscape, getting personal with audiences can make all the difference. Thus, making your content as relatable as possible on a personal level is key.

This is why sharing your personal experience with products is vital. When your audience sees that you have the first-hand experience with a product, they will know you're not just another peddler. Often, you see marketers talking about how much experience they have with certain products. So, they talk about how you can spot good ones from bad ones.

A good example of this is in the luxury watch niche. Experts spend time explaining to their audiences why certain watches are so expensive. Moreover, some will explain how to spot fake watches and so on. What you see here is experts sharing their experience with watches. This is what gives the credibility of their opinions.

So, don't be afraid to get personal. Try to relate your content to personal experience as much as possible. Your audience will appreciate that you are speaking from experience and not from a generic understanding of products.

Making Product Reviews Engaging

One of the most common ways in which affiliate marketers make money is through product reviews. These can be as superficial or thorough as you like. It's important to strike a balance. This means you don't want to dive too deep into a product, but you don't want to leave out pertinent information.

On the whole, a successful product review involves showing the product, talking about its distinct features, and the value it provides. Then, displaying the product in use is a great way to show your audience that you have experience with it. In this regard, you might use, wear, or otherwise put the product into action.

Depending on the nature of the product, you could live stream demonstrations. Also, you might have to produce several episodes so that audiences can see the full range of the products in action. As a result, your journey with the product can make your reviews highly engaging.

When it comes to experiences, such as travel, you may find it easy to compare hotels, restaurants, destinations, and so on. This will help audiences get a sense of the value they can derive from a given brand. Travel bloggers don't hold back. They show both good and bad when it comes to travel destinations, accommodation, and meals.

It's also important to be fair. There is no sense in trashing brands just because they are the competition. By the same token, there is no point in giving glowing reviews to a bad product. Acting in this manner will only damage your reputation. So, being objective and fair is the best way to build a credible reputation.

Use Reliable Sources

It's always a good idea to back up everything you say. While your audience will come to trust your opinion, backing up your claims with reliable sources will boost your credibility. Being an expert is one thing but providing evidence of your expertise takes everything to a whole new level.

For instance, when you deal with products related to nutrition, wellness, health, or fitness, it's a great idea to cite studies, articles, and other expert opinions. From this, audiences can see that you've done your homework. As such, you're not just ranting about what a good product something is. Audiences can see that you know what you're talking about. Plus, you have the integrity to back everything up.

Furthermore, backing up your claims makes you come across as authentic. There's nothing worse than watching videos or reading articles that are just one giant sales pitch. That's what TV commercials are for. In this case, your audience consumes your content because they feel they can get something useful from it.

A bold tactic some marketers use is to cite their competitors' claims. If you share the same opinion as your competitors, you can use this to back up your claims. So, rather than trashing your competition, you show that you're mature enough to give them credit when it's due.

Choose Products And Brands Carefully

Years of hard work can be trashed by a bad choice. For instance, if you choose a product that's bad, your audience may begin to question your integrity, knowledge, or expertise. The same goes for not doing your due diligence on product reviews. Your reputation can come into serious question if you give a positive review of a bad product.

In contrast, giving a bad review on a good product might make you seem like you have high standards. Of course, it depends on the nature of your critique. Still, making a harsh judgment on a good product may cause your audience to question your perspective.

One way of protecting yourself against undue criticism is to make your intentions clear. Often, this begins by stating that you stand to profit from sales of the product. Moreover, you ought to disclose any stake you have in the product itself. For instance, if you own the brand or make the products yourself, then audiences should be privy to that information. Otherwise, your audience might think you're trying to pull a fast one on them.

Additionally, try to avoid brands with shady reputations. Unless you're openly promoting such products, it's best to stay away from any products that you cannot vet. Taking a flyer on a new product may backfire. This is especially true if little is known about it. This is where the first-hand experience is key. You might be one of the first to review the product. As such, this needs to be communicated.

Develop A Consistent Approach

Your audience should see that type of criteria and standards you use to promote products. For example, you might be adamant about green products. So, you are clear on promoting environmentally-friendly products at all times. If you happen to promote an unsafe product, you might alienate some of your followers.

A consistent approach is based on communicating a philosophy. You can do this by simply stating what you like and don't like. Your audience will see that you are serious. So, flip-flopping your opinions won't help in the least bit.

If you are showcasing your skills, then it's important to develop a clear methodology. For example, if you are a do-it-yourselfer, then it's key that your audience sees you have a specific way of doing things. That is how they can see the effectiveness of the products you are promoting. Otherwise, experimenting with new gimmicks may backfire on you.

One approach that some influencers use is to let their imagination roam free. This approach can work depending on the nature of the products you are promoting. For instance, if you are looking to drive traffic to streaming sites, you might be able to get away with kooky antics. Also, some influencers go to outrageous lengths to promote a fashion brand. These tactics are valid so long as they resonate with your target audience.

Stay Current

Being outdated is a momentum killer. Users want fresh information on the newest trends. So, they may look to you as a source of updated information. This is why you need to stay on top of your respective niche. Depending on the niche, you may have to consistently update your information. In some cases, this might imply daily updates. Also, staying current with new product releases may require you to invest in purchasing new products before they are made available to the general public.

As you gain traction, don't be surprised if brands reach out to you before product launches. They may ask you to review their products in advance. Also, brands may provide you with all the information you need to make objective assessments of their products.

This is why you need to do your homework all the time. The last thing you want is to be caught with outdated information. Now, it's one thing to do poor research, and it's another to fall behind the competition. In the world of affiliate marketing, staying current is critical.

Sponsored Posts

If you have the opportunity to do sponsored posts, please bear in mind that you'll most likely have to give favorable reviews. This is a double-edged sword. On the one hand, you make money from these types of posts. On the other, your audiences may question your judgment. This is why it's necessary to be forthcoming in the event you are doing a sponsored post. Your audience is entitled to know that this is the case.

Nevertheless, successful affiliate marketers can make a lot of money from sponsored posts. Don't be afraid to take on these posts. However, make sure that you are dealing with reputable individuals. After all, if you get involved with questionable brands or companies, you might end up hurting your reputation.

Ultimately, making sponsored posts can become a great way to generate steady income. If you go down this route, you might want to explore another niche. That way, you can start over fresh if sponsored posts eventually dry up. Unfortunately, this is a reality in affiliate marketing. Success can be fleeting. So, it's a question of embracing it while it lasts.

Chapter 5:
Building An Online Presence

Affiliate marketing is all about creating an effective online presence. Besides great content, using the right platform can help you build the type of interaction you need to engage users. In contrast, the wrong approach to building your online presence can have detrimental consequences. This is why you need to consider all of the options available to you, so you can make the best decision.

Most affiliate marketers focus their efforts solely on social media. And while social media is certainly effective, there is only so much you can do with it. Eventually, social media will run its course. Thus, you need to have a presence across various media. That will allow you to heighten your reach. Moreover, you'll be able to reach your target market more effectively.

In this chapter, we're going to be looking at the various platforms that you can explore. We'll also discuss which ones fit better given the type of content present. In the end, the choice of a platform must consider the type of users you are looking to engage in. As you will see, you can make your presence felt across a myriad of media. Consequently, there is no need to focus yourself solely on social media.

Do take the time to ponder the best outlet to present your content. Please try to resist the temptation to copy what everyone else is doing. Keep in mind that what works for some doesn't necessarily work for others. You need to develop your style and presence. As a result, leveraging platforms to your advantage is a must.

Becoming A Blogger

Creating a blog is one of the first stops for affiliate marketers. By definition, blogs are text-heavy. This means that you can present a great deal of information to your followers. As such, a blog is a great way of providing consistent and highly detailed information.

Blogs are very useful especially since social media limits the amount of text you can present. Twitter only allows you 144 characters. Instagram isn't built for text. As for Facebook, overly long posts generally go unnoticed. Consequently, a blog makes sense if you are planning on providing copious amounts of information. Plus, you can organize information in a digestible manner. This not only facilitates understanding, but it also allows users to reference your material.

Travelers use blogs to chronicle their journeys. For instance, they use blogs to review destinations, hotels, airlines, and describe their experiences. Also, subject matter experts use blogs to provide users with detailed information. Virtually any professional can exploit a blog to their benefit. A blog can become a repository for reference information.

Platforms such as WordPress enable creators to embed various types of content. For instance, YouTube videos can fit in nicely. Additionally, social media sites can easily redirect traffic from a post to the blog. This strategy is often used. A social media post serves to entice users to visit the blog. There, they can find all the details on the topic.

If you are considering product reviews, offering expert advice, providing step-by-step instructions, or chronicling some kind of journey, then a blog is a great place to have as your starting point. From there, users can branch out to other platforms. In particular, your blog should contain links to all of your affiliate pages. Do not neglect to include as many links as possible.

Mailing Lists

Nowadays, most marketers neglect mailing lists. Often, they feel that mailing lists are outdated. However, they can be a great source of engagement especially if you can provide valuable content. Mailing lists can provide you with periodic contact with your users.

Due to regulations, you need to get users to sign up for your mailing list. To get users to willingly sign up, you need to provide them with content they can use. This generally comes in the form of a regular newsletter. Depending on your product, your newsletter can be daily, weekly, or monthly.

Once a user signs up, they get your content in their inbox. This content should compel them to visit any of your platforms. From there, they can hit any of your affiliate links. In some cases, marketers openly suggest users visit their affiliates straight from their inbox.

Building mailing lists takes time. It usually implies building a strong following across various platforms. For instance, you can produce content for YouTube and ask viewers to sign up for your mailing list. The same can be done on social media. From a social media post, users can be redirected to your sign-up page.

The only problem with mailing lists is to avoid spamming. If you send out content too frequently, you may end up turning off your users. So, it's best to email less frequently than you'd like. Here are some examples to consider:

- If you deal with products that folks regularly consume (cosmetics, food and drink, clothes, shoes, entertainment) you can try emailing daily.

- News outlets and publishers often email daily (once a day only)

- Luxury goods email weekly or twice a month.

- Niche products (those that have a very specific market) email less frequently

- Entertainers email very frequently (music and movie streaming sites, for instance)

Based on these guidelines, you can assess where you stand. Please bear in mind that if your product has a high turnover, then you might consider upping the frequency of your contact. The last thing you want to do is tire your users. So, it's best to start slow and ramp up your contact rather than having to scale back.

Social Media

Just about every marketer starts with social media. Logic dictates that social media should be the starting point for any successful digital marketing endeavor. However, those that swear by social media learn that the internet is a vast expanse. As such, limiting yourself to social media is very narrow-minded.

The purpose of social media is to create engagement. This type of engagement should compel your users to follow you, which then leads to your users hitting those affiliate links. Often, this might mean hitting the links straight from your social media pages or visiting your blog.

Social media is also great if you are looking to promote other platforms. This type of cross-selling is great because it allows you to keep your users hopping from one place to another. This is important because practically all users have some kind of presence across various platforms. So, you might find they spend time on YouTube, Facebook, and Twitter. Thus, linking your users across various platforms is a great way of keeping engagement up.

So, let's take a look at how you can leverage the various social media platforms out there.

Facebook

Nowadays, Facebook is seen as a classic. It's a staple of social media. However, it is no longer the hottest place to be. Facebook is still quite popular with the older crowd. Please bear in mind that Facebook was the only show in town for a while. Therefore, a vast number of users became accustomed to Facebook. As more platforms emerged (such as Snapchat or Instagram), younger users preferred these to Facebook.

Facebook is a great platform when you have a balanced approach between text and image. If your marketing endeavors target older audiences, and you present a text-image combo, then Facebook is a good place to start. However, avoid long texts as much as possible. Extremely long texts (anything beyond 150 words) will not compel users to read them. The most successful posts use 50 words or less.

Additionally, Facebook makes a great trampoline. From here, you can get users to visit your Instagram, YouTube, Snapchat, or Twitter sites. Plus, you can use it to redirect users to affiliate links, blogs, or online shops.

Instagram

Instagram is image heavy. This means that images say it all. This is why fashion brands exploit Instagram. Influencers also make a living out of it. If you are looking to promote anything in the world of fashion, lifestyle, travel, or experiences, Instagram is the place to be. It's also the place to be when looking to access a younger demographic.

Using short video clips is also a very useful technique on Instagram. Short clips can be used to send a message or present a call to action. Instagram can also be used to redirect users to affiliate links. However, it doesn't work quite as well as a trampoline. So, don't be afraid to ask users to visit your affiliate links rather than your blog or website.

Tik Tok

Tik Tok is a relative newcomer to the scene. However, its popularity has been meteoric. It is used by influencers that like to maintain a consistent presence in the minds of their followers. You can use this platform if you need an alternative to Instagram. Moreover, it's a hit with teenagers. Hence, if your products are directed at teenagers, Tik Tok is the place to be.

To succeed on this platform, you ought to show your products in action. Any product works as long as you can produce a short clip depicting your product in action. However, try to avoid much of the silliness that you see on this platform. You want to make sure that your users keep their eyes on the ball the whole time.

Twitter

Twitter is text heavy. This is a great platform for those seeking to maintain a great deal of contact with their followers. Publishers, news media, and highly influential individuals use

Twitter frequently. Given the restrictive nature of 144 characters, you need to be precise in what you say. As such, Twitter can be a great complement to other social media sites. You can leverage Twitter as a means of staying on top of the game. If you are providing content that your users need to know right away, Twitter is the place to be. Everything from celebrity gossip to the latest product releases is a fair game on Twitter. Additionally, Twitter can be a great alternative to mailing lists.

Reddit and Quora

These sites don't get as much attention as they should. These sites are text intensive. So, they are great for people seeking very specific information. You can build a presence here especially if you are an expert in your field. You might find it interesting to see people seeking your advice. That is why using threads on these sites can provide you with the opportunity to redirect users to your blog, website, or YouTube. However, sending them to social media may defeat the purpose of a purely text-based interaction.

Video Streaming

YouTube is the king of video streaming. Virtually anyone who's anyone needs a YouTube channel. Since YouTube is imminently visual, it is a great platform for anyone looking to do product reviews and demos. It's also great for anyone looking to provide exposure to brands.

However, YouTube is also used by podcasters. You should not overlook this alternative. For those types of products that allow for deep discussion, creating YouTube-based podcasts makes sense. For instance, experts, commentators, and analysts use YouTube as a means of providing in-depth information. YouTube can also provide a visual alternative to blogging.

Hence, the concept of a "vlog" can go hand in hand with a regular blog.

Educational companies use the blog-YouTube combo to engage users across multiple levels. Fashion brands use YouTube quite a bit though it isn't as successful as Instagram. Also, if you are looking to show your products in real-life action, then YouTube is the place to be.

Also, YouTube is not the only show in town. Vimeo, Patreon, and BitChute can all provide you with great alternatives to YouTube. Of course, YouTube is mass media at its best. However, it's also worth exploring other alternatives especially if you find that your users also interact with sites other than YouTube.

Please bear in mind that a successful YouTube strategy is based on delivering fresh content regularly. Therefore, you need to keep your game up especially if you are trying to hit a younger demographic.

Chapter 6:
Best Sites For Affiliate Marketing

The core of affiliate marketing is finding the right affiliate sites to work with. There are many potential sites you can sign up with. Some are big box sites like Amazon while others may be specific to a brand. The point is to find the sites that best reflect what you are trying to achieve. In this regard, you ought to look for the sites that offer you the highest commissions and flexible payouts.

It's also important to note that not all affiliates are created equal. Some sites offer a no-hassle approach while others make it a bit harder. This is why finding a solid affiliate site can provide you with the right opportunities to make a reasonable income.

In this chapter, we're going to be looking at the best sites you can sign up with. These sites will provide you with the best chances of making a reasonable income right from the start. Best of all, most of these sites offer no-hassle sign up. So, all you have to do is sign up and get the ball rolling.

Amazon Associates

It makes sense to start with Amazon. It's the biggest e-commerce site in the world. It's also the most popular place for affiliate marketers to make the bulk of their earnings. Furthermore, Amazon is known all over the world. So, your chance of making money is multiplied when working with Amazon.

On the whole, Amazon is great because you can earn up to 10% on all qualified sales. While the overall rate may vary from product to product, you'll still have a chance to earn a decent commission. It's always best to make sure you check how much you stand to earn.

Another great aspect about Amazon is that any purchases made on the site that come from your link (even if they are not the ones you signed up for) count toward your commission payout. Plus, their sheer variety of products available on Amazon make it the easiest place to make money.

On the flip side, your referrals only have 24 hours to make a purchase. So, if a user clicks on your link, they have 24 hours to make a purchase. If they purchase after 24 hours, you don't qualify for the payout. Also, Amazon doesn't have many payment options. You need to get paid by check, bank deposit, or through gift cards. Amazon doesn't use any digital payment service. That might be an issue for you.

eBay Partners

eBay is highly diverse. The number of products sold across categories makes it Amazon's biggest rival. eBay is powered by individual users. Thus, practically anybody can sell their wares on eBay. As such, you can also make money by promoting specific posts. Mainly, these posts are related to products that are related to your content. Thus, eBay is a great alternative to Amazon. As a matter of fact, most marketers include eBay and Amazon links in their content.

eBay is great for niche products. This is especially true if you are dealing with antiques, rare collectibles, or looking to deal with international suppliers. Consequently, eBay provides a good deal of diversity. With eBay partners, you find rather straightforward rules. This means that there are no complex guidelines to uphold. Lastly, you get a double commission for the first three months. So, it pays to blow your eBay referral out of the water.

On the downside, you get zilch if an auction takes over 10 days to end even if the winning bidder comes through your link. Also, you must share your commission along with eBay. This happens because eBay gets a cut of whatever the seller makes. So, you split that cut with eBay. While you get the most of it, you don't get to keep all of it.

Shopify Affiliates

Shopify is great because it allows regular folks to set up their online shop. It provides folks with all the tools they need to make money selling online. Those tools include referral programs. Bloggers and online merchants are quite familiar with it.

You can earn quite a bit using Shopify. For starters, you get your referral's first two monthly payments (roughly $200) and up to $598 on a standard plan. You can also earn up to $2,000 on an enterprise plan. The great thing about Shopify is that it pays out well given that it's the leader in its class. However, please bear in mind that Shopify caters to a very specific market. Hence, your sales may not be nearly as high. Still, the payout cannot be ignored.

Rakuten Affiliates

Rakuten caters mainly to Asian markets though it has a global presence. If your content manages to reach a truly global audience, it makes sense to sign up for Rakuten. This would give your customers in overseas markets the chance to find your products.

The good thing about Rakuten is that it is a trusted brand throughout the world. It has large partnerships with organizations such as the NBA. It's a recognizable brand. The bad thing is that you must apply for individual brands. This isn't a sweeping account like Amazon or eBay. As such, you need to work directly with brands. You can't simply promote products in general. That's why it pays to be familiar with individual brands.

Clickbank

'Clickbank' is a site that groups merchants from all over the world. As such, there is always something to promote. While it's not quite as big as Amazon, it's a great secondary strategy. Generally speaking, 'Clickbank' can provide you with alternative opportunities to merchants that may not qualify for Amazon, or that would rather not play by Amazon's rules.

The sheer diversity of merchants alone is enough to entice content creators to sign up with 'Clickbank'. Their signup process is hassle-free. So, you won't have become frustrated by their politics. On the downside, their sales are capped off at $150. Thus, the most you could earn on an individual sale is $150. That might sound like a bit of a turnoff. Again, 'Clickbank' is a great secondary strategy. It can help complement your earnings from other sites.

ShareASale

This site works similarly to 'Clickbank'. There are a host of merchants promoting all sorts of products. As a result, you won't have to turn over stones to find products you can promote. It's rather easy to get started with them, too.

The best part about 'ShareASale' is that it has flexible payout alternatives. This is a combination of digital payment options and regular ones. So, you can find a great way of putting together your finances. The only downer with 'ShareASale' is that you do need some technical knowledge to sign up. If you know your way around computers, it shouldn't be a hassle. But for some technologically challenged folks, it might be a bit complex.

Solvid Affiliates

Solvid is a European-based affiliate platform. Thus, it makes sense to work with them if you live in Europe. Alternatively, if your content manages to hit overseas users, then you need this. Moreover, Solvid and Rakuten make sense if you are planning a global approach.

This is the highest paying program in the market. Affiliates can earn up to 20% on individual sales. There is no cap or limit. So, if a referral goes off the deep end, you'll cash in. It's a straightforward system to sign up for. There doesn't seem to be any downsides to it. As a result, it's certainly worth working with Solvid.

Google AdSense

Google AdSense is not an affiliate program in the traditional sense. However, it's the best way for bloggers and publishers to make money. The way it works is that your users will see ads on your site. So, when they click on the ad, they'll be referred to that merchant. Therefore, it works under the same principles through which your users won't find links to affiliate sites.

On the whole, AdSense is a good option. There is no need to promote individual products. You can also choose what types of ads can be displayed. However, you don't have any control over which ads are shown. So, this might upset some of your users. Nevertheless, it provides you with a means of monetizing a blog or site. It also works well in tandem with YouTube (YouTube is a Google-owned company).

Choosing The Best Affiliate Site

The options discussed in this chapter are all great ones to choose from. They can help you hit the ground running. Mainly, you won't have to go through hoops to sign up. Naturally, it takes time to build a following. Still, you can start making money right from the start. This is why these sites are a great way to see your hard work pay off.

On the whole, most successful marketers work with eBay and Amazon and then branch out into other sites. It's also worth trying out various sites to see which ones work best with your brands, products, and users. In the end, you have a wide selection of affiliates. So, there's no need to depend on a single program.

Chapter 7:
Introduction To Search Engine Optimization

Search Engine Optimization, or SEO, is a technique that's used to position in content concerning search results in search engines. Search Engines (like Google, Bing, DuckDuckGo, among others) are used to search for content based on a query conducted by a user. This query can come in the form of a question like, "what is the nearest dry cleaner?" or it can be based on keywords like, "dry cleaner New York."

When a user types in the words in a query, the results returned by the search engine reveal the most relevant results. It's important to note that relevant search results are based on the content within the website and not the quality of the content itself. This means that content can be a bunch of gibberish, but if it's written based on SEO principles, then it has a greater likelihood of popping up at the top of search results.

There's also something important to consider when it comes to SEO: sites get placed at the top of search results based on the number of hits they get. This means that the more traffic a site gets, the higher its position atop search results. This is why traffic is just as important as the content itself.

In this chapter, we are going to discuss the fundamentals of SEO and how you can take full advantage of it when designing your content. That way, you can position yourself right where users can see you.

Fundamentals Of SEO

Generally speaking, SEO tactics center around cramming a certain set of keywords into content as much as possible. This tactic is certainly useful. However, it is not the only one. That's why understanding the full picture will enable you to position your content atop of search results.

Within the SEO domain, there is a hierarchy for content. This hierarchy is like a pyramid that ranks content. When your content sits at the top of this pyramid, it will be highly visible. This is important particularly when you're dealing with rather generic products. Unless you specialize in a very narrow niche, or you have distinctive qualities in your content, you need to have SEO on your side.

Let's look at this hierarchy:

1. **Crawl accessibility**. Search engines can "read" the content on your site, blog, or webpage.

2. **Compelling material**. Your material provides the answers to specific questions.

3. **Keyword heavy**. Your content is filled with the keyword's users are likely to search for.

4. **User experience**. Great user experience is based on fast loading times and ease of use.

5. **Great content**. This means you have "share-worthy" content such as those on social media.

6. **Click-through rates**. Titles, URLs, and descriptions all provide ample information including the use of keywords.

7. **Snippets or schema results**. These are the pages that the search engine presents users based on query results.

When your content can hit the top of the hierarchy, that is numbers 6 and 7, then you know you are on top of your game. This is why we're going to discuss each of these aspects in greater detail.

Crawl Accessibility

Crawl accessibility is the first level of the SEO hierarchy. In essence, it relates to the ability that search engines have to "read" your content. In other words, your content needs to be set up in such a way that search engines can index it. By "index," we're talking about register its existence.

When talking about crawl accessibility we are, by no means, talking about hitting the top of search results. Unless a user types in the exact words on your URL, blog title, or even your name, you may not appear within the first few pages of search results.

It's important to note that most users will not look at search results beyond the first page. If you can't make it on to the first page of search results, you practically don't exist. Therefore, you must improve upon this level.

Also, it's important to consider that just creating a website on its own won't get you noticed. You'll need to take action to get noticed. So, here are three steps you can take to put your content on the map.

1. **Send a sitemap to Google**. If you are creating a website, then submitting your sitemap to Google will formally register you on the search. Again, this doesn't

mean you'll be at the top, but at least you're on the horizon.

2. **Create links across various platforms**. If you have a site, blog, YouTube channel, and so on, linking them across various platforms helps. As such, the more places links to your content appears, the more chances search engines have in discovering you.

3. **Update regularly**. When sites aren't updated regularly, they get cold. This means that the lack of updates on the site pushes them down the SEO ranks. So, updating regularly will keep you fresh in the search engine's minds.

Compelling Material

When you think of compelling material, you think of content your users find interesting and useful. Naturally, this is the essence of the content you provide. However, it's important to make this content compelling to search engines as well. Considering that users generally search for content based on queries (questions), then your content needs to answer specific questions that users may use to find content related to your domain.

For instance, if you have a car blog, you might consider answering the question, "what is the best car brand?" To do this, you can create a post with this specific title. Also, you can include this question in a social media post, YouTube video, or Twitter thread. That way, search engines will pick up on the exact word's users would use to search.

Additionally, the use of hashtags helps. Hashtags help searchability especially when your strategy is social media heavy. Please bear in mind that the more mentions or references there are to your material, the greater the likelihood you'll be at the top of searches.

Keyword Heavy

The segue to compelling material is the heavy use of keywords. Keywords are based on the term's users are likely to use. The more of these terms your content contains, the higher your ranking on search results. Copywriters that specialize in SEO build content around keywords. So, rather than having content including keywords, content is created around specific search terms.

The best place to start is with titles. Blogs and social media posts that contain keywords help tremendously. Furthermore, YouTube video titles and descriptions containing keywords make a world of difference.

It's worth noting that you should take advantage of any means you have to include text containing keywords. Don't neglect description boxes, profiles, or any other means of including keywords. To define the keywords that you will use, simply think about the type of users you want to attract. Additionally, think about keywords that are linked to your products. That way, you make it easier for users to find you.

Once you have given that thought. Type it into that specific search engine and see if it comes up with the most relevant and most popular items relating to your search. If it does then that is now what you would call a good keyword.

Do this multiple times with multiple keywords to get the best results. It's a bit of trial and error but it is defiantly worth your time to do so.

User Experience

The big winner here is load times. Search engines can track how long it takes your site to load. Therefore, a slower load time (usually due to heavy graphic use) can negatively impact your search rankings.

To improve your ranking, strive to make your content as easy to load as possible. Going for the leanest layout is the best way to go. To achieve this, try to avoid heavy graphics or multimedia content on your homepage. You can provide all of this content in other parts of your site. In the meantime, try to keep it simple yet precise.

Another important aspect of user experience is mobile responsiveness. This means that your site (including social media platforms) should be mobile-friendly. As a result, ensuring that you have a fully functioning mobile version of your site is a must.

Lastly, search engines also track the number of hits and average time users spend on your site. The number of individual hits counts greatly. However, the average time users spend on your content plays an even bigger role. In short, the longer users spend on your site, the higher your rankings.

Great Content

When you have great content, it usually gets shared. In essence, the more shares your content gets, the greater the impact it has on search results. This applies to all social media platforms. Moreover, if users post your links on multiple social media platforms, then you have a great shot at climbing the rankings.

Some dishonest folks cheat the system by creating a bunch of fake profiles. These "users" share content on Facebook, Instagram, Twitter, and YouTube. This artificially inflates share rates thereby boosting searchability. Social media platforms have cracked down on this over the years. However, social media algorithms don't have a way of knowing who's a fake unless there are red flags such as cloned profiles.

On the whole, asking your users to share your content certainly helps in this regard. This is why you hear YouTubers say, "please like, share and subscribe" all the time. The reason they always say that is to boost their searchability.

Another useful tactic is to crosslink your content across platforms. Now, this goes beyond simply posting links on various platforms. This is about getting users to hop from one site to another. For instance, you redirect users from your Facebook profile to your Instagram. Also, you redirect users from Instagram to YouTube. This type of hopping is highly visible by search engines. Unless your users are surfing in anonymous mode, their movements will show up. So, this certainly bodes well for your search results.

Click-through Rates

This is a rather straightforward concept. Yet, it is one of the most powerful. Click-through rates mean the number of users that click on your links, ads, or posts. So, the more users that click on your links, the greater your visibility. However, this is easier said than done.

In the olden days, click-through rates were measured by banner ads. Nowadays, click-through rates are measured by the number of times people engage with your content. Therefore, you will find that marketers post several links in the description of every social media post. By doing this, they can amplify the reach of their content. Naturally, all links have content linked to one another. Thus, if a user visits a YouTube channel, the links provided in the description can then lead users to blogs, sites, or other social media pages.

If you sign up for affiliate schemes in which you get paid on a per-click basis, then this is where you need to be. To enhance your click ability, you need to make it easy for your users to hit those links. To start, your content should compel users to hit on your links. Furthermore, users should be incentivized. Therefore, you should offer specific content across your entire presence. Simply posting the same content across all platforms is not going to get your noticed. Please bear in mind that having your users hopping from one site to another is the best way to improve your visibility.

Snippets or Schema Results

Snippets are short summaries that appear on search results. These are the ultimate as users can preview your content before clicking on it. There are two ways in which you can get your snippet atop search results. One, you can have a sponsored link. Two, your content gets insane traffic.

Google uses AdSense as a means of advertising. You can pay for a certain amount of exposure based on the demographic you are looking to reach. Then, your site appears based on search terms. This may seem like a bit of an unfair advantage. When you consider the cost of using AdSense, it's hardly fair.

The second way to get your snippets out is to have insane traffic. Sites that get thousands of hits a day will get this type of exposure. This is why constantly updating content is crucial to achieving this type of searchability.

Now, if you can't update your content multiple times a day, at least try to be as consistent as you can. If that means updating content three times a week, then try your best to stick to that tempo. The longer you go without updating content, the colder your searchability will get.

Chapter 8:
Leveraging Social Media

Using social media in affiliate marketing is a no-brainer. If you have no presence on social media, you don't exist. This is why successful marketers build a presence across all relevant social media platforms. To do this, they build a strategy. This means that they don't haphazardly post content. As a matter of fact, the worst thing you can do is create content that's just repeated across various platforms. This type of action does not incentivize users to visit their various platforms.

In this chapter, we are going to look at building a social media strategy that incorporates all platforms regardless of the product or service you are promoting. Please bear in mind that you should strive to create content that can only be accessed by visiting that platform. In short, if they don't follow you on the X, Y, or Z platform, they are missing out.

Defining a Social Media Strategy

When going about your social media strategy, you need to incorporate all of the elements we have described throughout this book. This means defining your niche market, target users, and products. Having this clearly defined will enable you to focus on the social media platforms that will provide the most value.

Here are a couple of rules to keep in mind:

- For younger users, Instagram, YouTube, Snapchat, and Tik Tok are the most popular.

- For older users, Facebook, LinkedIn, YouTube, and Twitter all make the most sense.

However, there is no need to limit yourself to a given set of platforms. What this means is that you will focus the bulk of your efforts on the most effective sites. If you can link your content to all platforms, then you'll have an outstanding chance to make serious headway.

The main idea here is to offer content that users would not be able to access otherwise. In doing so, you incentivize your users to hop from one platform to another. Consider this example:

You promote several jewelry brands. So, you are casting a rather wide net as you seek to capture both younger and older users. This means that you are compelled to use a sweeping strategy across all possible platforms.

Your core strategy is based on a YouTube channel. In this channel, you post regular product reviews and tryouts. You ask your users to follow you on Instagram. There, they can get a glimpse of your products in real-life action. Also, you ask your viewers to follow you on Facebook. Here, you post pictures of your products along with descriptions and reviews while encouraging your users to leave comments and questions. To further increase your reach, you have a blog in which you write longer posts about your life and how your products are a part of your regular, day-to-day life.

As you can see, building an overarching strategy across various platforms makes sense. This allows you to engage users at various levels. Plus, you can incorporate other types of social media platforms like Tik Tok or even LinkedIn. It might sound surprising, but you shouldn't limit your scope to just one or two platforms. Please remember that the more presence you can maintain, the greater your chances of hitting one out of the ballpark.

Getting Started

Depending on your products and audiences, your starting point may change. Therefore, you might have a visual-heavy strategy centered around YouTube and Instagram. Or, you might have a more text-heavy approach based on a blog, Facebook, Twitter.

Whatever you determine to be your starting point, this needs to be the core of your content. For instance, if you decide that your core is a blog, then all of your content needs to point toward that blog. As such, Facebook and Twitter posts should include links to your products, and most importantly, to your blog.

On the other hand, if you have a visual-heavy approach, you may choose to build your strategy around Instagram. Here, you can post pictures and stories throughout the week. In each post, you encourage users to visit your links and/or your YouTube channel. There, they will find exclusive content they can't find anywhere else. Repetition is key here, the more you constantly tell someone to go to a link. Eventually they will go there out of curiosity, if they are following you.

Please note that whatever your core platform is, you need to build all of your efforts around it. In this regard, you can create the following based on your target audience. You can incorporate other platforms to improve your visibility, though you can't be sure that these other platforms will not provide you with the same reach.

To define your core platform, please refer to the steps in identifying your target audience. Then, take a look at the references we have provided for engaging older and younger audiences.

Posting Content

When building your social media strategy, you should strive to create a narrative across your platforms. This may include creating a persona and lifestyle. While we are not advocating a false facade, you may find it useful to tell a story that isn't exactly your real life. After all, we are all entitled to a private life away from the public.

In this regard, creating a narrative is vital. That way, users can feel there is a logical thread to everything you post. In a manner of speaking, it's like creating a TV series. You keep users tuned in hoping to learn more about each of the characters and see where the story is going.

Furthermore, posting content as often as possible will keep audiences coming back for more. Depending on the type of products you are pitching, your content may be posted several times a day. However, if you are going at it solo, you may find it hard to post content regularly. So, you might strive to post something new every day.

This is where presence across various platforms works.

For example, Twitter is quite easy to use frequently. You can post several times a day on Twitter. Then, you may choose to post a new picture on Instagram every day while posting on Facebook three or four times a week. If you are producing content for YouTube, you might find it useful to have your content there at least a couple of times a week.

The key here is to be consistent. The more often you post content, the better you can engage your audiences. Make sure you become familiar with the various metrics that social media platforms use. They will tell you if you are overdoing it or if you need to ramp things up.

For instance, if you are getting a consistent number of hits, you choose to up your content, and then your engagement drops, then you are overdoing it or your putting up bad quality content. By the same token, if you post, then get a large number of hits, and then your engagement falls off a cliff, you're not posting enough. You will find the "goldilocks zone" when you find that your content gets a consistent amount of hits. Its merely a matter of regulating the responses. It may also help to write down how many views/likes you get per week.

Case Study

Let's look at a practical example that encompasses everything we're talked about in this chapter.

Mary is a schoolteacher who has decided to give affiliate marketing a go. She specializes in teaching math. So, she has decided to build her strategy around helping kids to improve their math skills. As such, she is targeting a double-whammy audience. On the one hand, she's targeting the kids that will consume her educational content while also targeting parents.

Mary has chosen YouTube as her core. She plans to post content three times a week. This decision is based on the amount of time she can reasonably devote to producing content given her current lifestyle.

Next, she has chosen to use Facebook, Instagram, Twitter, and build a blog.

In the blog, Mary posts links and resources to books, free online resources, and other useful materials. She openly promotes certain book publishers. She uses their materials to teach math. So, parents are encouraged to visit the sites of these publishers so they can purchase any materials they wish. Mary ensures to provide links in her blog posts.

Also, Mary adds links to her Facebook and Instagram profiles. On Facebook, she posts shorts clips in which she answers a specific question posed by one of her students. Links to her YouTube videos are included. Besides, she asks users to check out her Instagram profile. On Instagram, Mary showcases a bit more of her personal life. This may include bits about her day-to-day life, pics with her students, or simply talking about anything not related to math.

Then, Mary uses Twitter to provide tips, comments, or any other relevant information to math, or that may be of interest to students and parents. She encourages users to visit her YouTube channel while also referring users to her blog.

To maximize her SEO visibility, Mary makes sure to pack as many keywords as she can into her content. For example, she commonly titles her blog posts in the form of a question like, "how to calculate square roots?" Or, "What's a second-degree function?" These blog posts are popular with students because they receive step-by-step instructions. As for parents, they also benefit from these posts.

Bringing it All Together

As you can see, Mary has a fully integrated social media strategy. She mainly promotes books, courses, or online learning platforms. She has partnerships with Amazon, eBay, and individual book publishers. In the end, she makes some extra income based on something she does for a living.

The best part of Mary's strategy is that she's focusing her efforts on providing value to her students. Moreover, she has found a way to also engage parents. Looking toward the future, she's thinking about producing her line of online courses and books. These are meant to provide her with an additional source of income and exposure.

As long as you put thought into building your strategy, you'll have a coherent approach that can lead you to achieve your aims. The last thing you want to do is improvise. Often, you may have to about things through trial and error. As such, if something doesn't work as you had planned, it's alright. You can always go back to the drawing board. The key is to maintain a coherent narrative that your audience can relate to. In the end, this will be your biggest key to success.

Conclusion

Thank you for making it through to the end of this volume. I hope you enjoyed learning the ins and outs of different media platforms. Analyze your topic or niche thoroughly. Decipher which platforms will be best suited using the information you have obtained today and get started.

Please be proactive in marketing what it is your willing to sell. The more you contemplate something and not do it the more you will not ever do it.

Take action and 'Do IT'

Finally, if you found this book useful in any way, a positive review on Amazon is always appreciated!

Good luck with your new online business!

www.ingramcontent.com/pod-product-compliance
Lightning Source LLC
Chambersburg PA
CBHW070501220526
45466CB00004B/1915